D0789724

3

Migration

Illustrated by Carol Tyler

Nelson

spring summer

autumn winter

Migrate means to move from one place
to another.
Many animals migrate.
They come and go with the seasons
of the year.
This is called migration.

Whales and seals are two mammals
that migrate.
Hump-backed whales live near the south pole.
They go to warmer water to have their babies.
Seals spend most of their time out at sea.
They go to the same place every year
where the young seals are born on land.

Eels that live in rivers and ponds migrate
when they are old.
They travel to the Sargasso Sea.
They lay eggs in the deep salt water
and then die.
The baby eels migrate back again.

The salmon is another fish that migrates.
Unlike the eel, it goes from
salt to fresh water.
The salmon swim up rivers to lay eggs.
Sometimes it is hard work!
The baby salmon migrate back to the sea.

Many insects migrate.

Locusts migrate in millions, eating everything as they go.

Many kinds of butterflies migrate too.

In some parts of the world they can seem to fill the whole sky.

Painted Lady

Monarch

Red Admiral

locust

Things to do and talk about

1   Which of these words remind you
    of migration?

    Write the words.

    swarm   nesting   holiday   flock
    aeroplane   journey   seasons   message

2   Here are some animals which migrate:

    Which animal do you like best? Why?
    Talk or write about it.

3   Pretend you have seen a cloud
    of butterflies migrating.
    Say how it looked and how you felt.

4   People migrate too.

The map shows three places in the world to which many people have migrated.

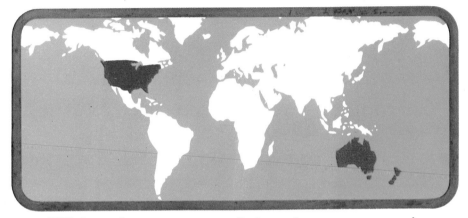

Write the names of the three countries which are in colour.

5   What am I?

I live in the sea. I am very big.
I have live babies. I migrate.
Draw me. Write my name.

© Leonard Sealey 1973
© Illustrations Thomas Nelson & Sons Ltd 1973
Published by Thomas Nelson & Sons Ltd,
36 Park Street, London W1Y 4DE
First published 1973
Printed in Great Britain by Colour Reproductions, Billericay, Essex
0 17 422222 X

One bird migrates further than all the rest.
It is the arctic tern.
It migrates almost halfway round
the world.
The arctic tern flies from near
the north pole to near the south pole.
The flight takes two or three months.

Some birds migrate in the day-time.
These are the fast fliers who eat insects
as they go.
Most small birds migrate at night.
They eat in the day-time and fly
when the sun sets.

We know how far some birds migrate.
Birds are caught before they fly away.
Rings are put on their legs.
The birds are then set free.
When the birds have migrated,
the rings show where they came from.

The swallows, that are in England in summer, migrate to South Africa.
The cuckoo flies to Africa, too.

Cuckoos lay their eggs in other birds' nests.
So baby cuckoos do not live with their parents.
They have to find their own way to Africa.

Many kinds of birds migrate all over
the world.
Millions of them move from where
the baby birds were born.
Great flocks of birds migrate together.
They fly away for the winter and come back
in the spring.

A bird is very light in weight.
The bones of a bird are hollow.
You know how light feathers are.
Birds have strong wings.
So many birds can keep flying
for a very long time.

Many animals that migrate
go a very long way.
They move hundreds or thousands
of kilometres.
It can take them a long time.
The animals seem to know where to go.
Nobody really knows how they find
their way.

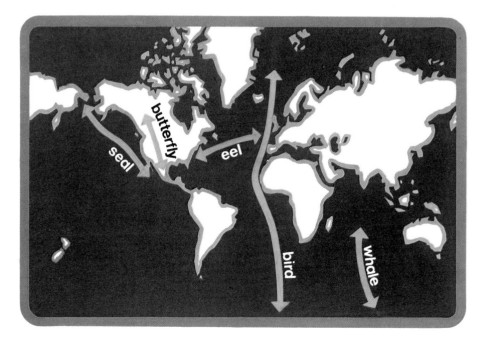

Some animals migrate because the weather
changes.
They move to places where it is easier
to find food.
Many animals migrate to have their babies.
This gives the babies the best chance
to grow up.

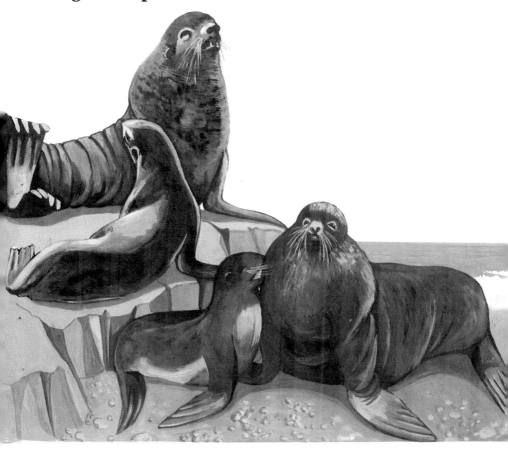